MALHAR RAMCHARRAN&
DR. RAM P. RAMCHARRAN

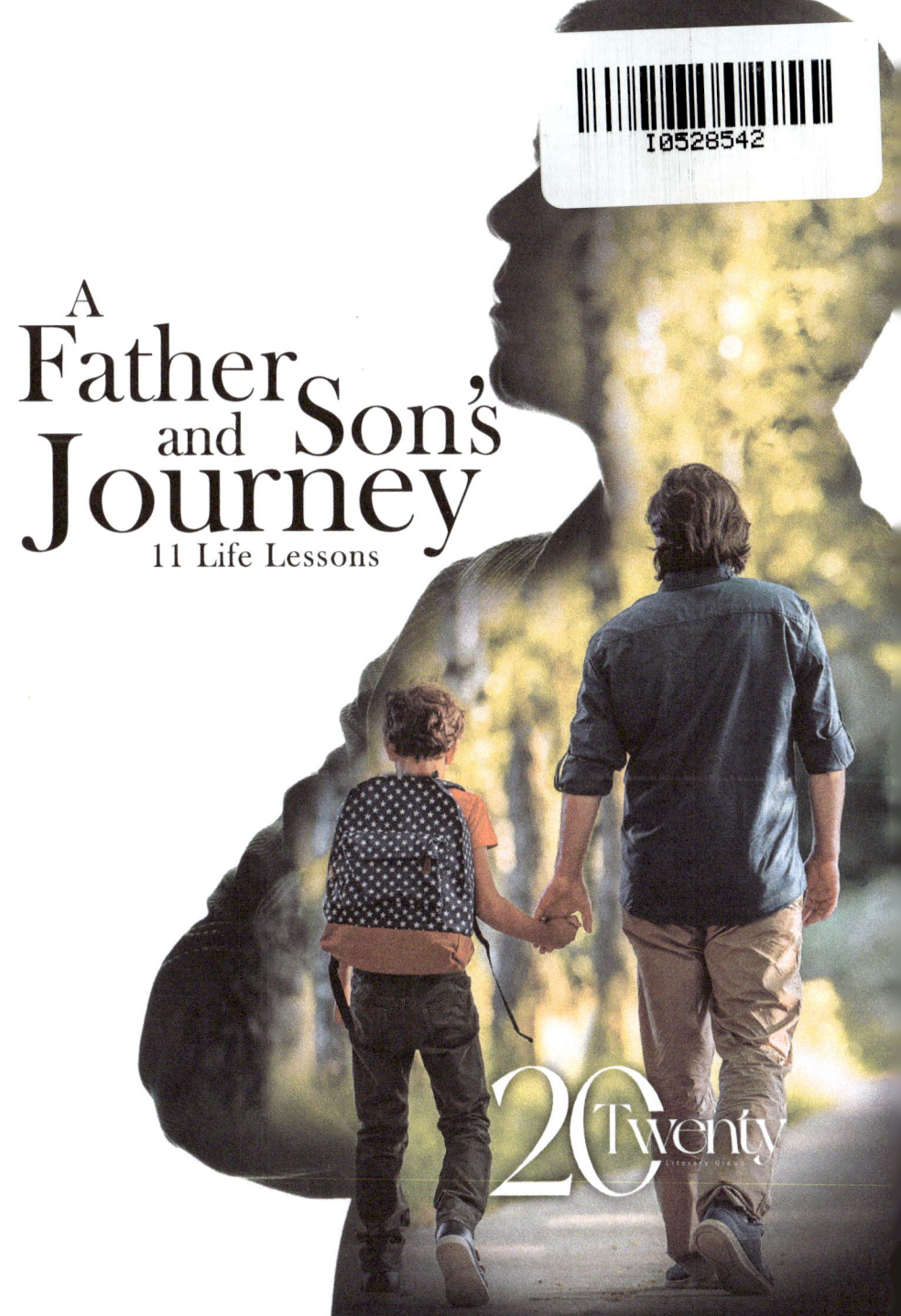

A
Father
and Son's
Journey
11 Life Lessons

20 Twenty
Literary Group

A Father and Son's Journey
Copyright © 2024 by Malhar Ramcharran & Dr. Ram P. Ramcharran

ISBN
978-1-962868-50-1 (Paperback)
978-1-962868-51-8 (eBook)
978-1-964488-04-2 (Hardcover)

Dedicated

To Sadhana & To Mom

Table of Contents

Forewords

In this heart-warming and inspiring book, A father and son shares their story, journey, and passion for life, they reflect on the circumstances and events which have Cris-crossed their lives. The father is a successful businessman, while his son is a free-spirited creator who follows his heart. As they journey through life together, they learn to overcome challenges, build trust, and find common ground even in times of crisis and heartache.

Through their experiences, the father and son come to realize that it's okay to be different. They learn that everyone has something unique to offer, and that diversity is a strength. They also learn that challenges can be overcome with love, patience, and understanding.

The most important lesson that the father and son learn is the importance of looking at life from the prism of love. When they see the world through the eyes of love, they can find beauty and meaning in even the most difficult situations. They are also able to forgive each other's mistakes and appreciate each other's strengths.

This book is a reminder that love is the most powerful force in the world. It can help us overcome any challenge and find true happiness. It is a story that will stay with you long after you finish reading it.

By
Sesh Sukhdeo, MBA

Acknowledgments

We would like to thank our family for the help and contribution in making this book possible. Without the stories and lesson coming from them and being part of the process, it would not be possible to write it.

We would like to thank Sadhana Ramcharran for giving us all those years of great lessons, memories and for her love and understanding for all those years.

We like to thank our family members Agee, Vidita, Rohan, Feindy, and Shivani for giving us their love, passion and understanding. We would like to thank everyone who has provided us with insight and sharing knowledge over the years, with all the help we have gained valuable lessons we can share with all you.

Malhar & Dr. Ram P. Ramcharran

Introduction

This book offers 11 life lessons that a Dad shared with his son as a way to bond. Dad shares his lessons and experiences with his son and his son shares his lessons and experiences back as he has encountered in his life to date. In edition II of 11 life Lessons, you experience with the updated stories shared how Malhar has matured and how he has been able to handle his challenges. It's a delightful, honest and heart felt sharing of Malhar's emotions and experience. This self-help, self-improvement story book is fun and easy to read and can serve as a simple handbook that can be shared from parents to their children to help them better understand each other. The stories shared are real and are full of emotions and life experiences both from Malhar and Dr. Ramcharran.

Using real-life experiences and anecdotes, this book provides an easy to read and understand guide for helping young people find purpose and recognizing true potential in life. In this book, authors Dr. Ram Ramcharran and Malhar Ramcharran, share life experience from two periods in this updated addition when Malhar was only 11 years old and now 18, you can see with these 11 life lessons showing how it has impacted their lives and you can see how these experience were handled and dealt with as Malhar and his dad grew as individuals and as a family. Readers will be able to use these 11 rules and lessons shared to improve their life and relationship with their children.

Malhar and Dr. Ramcharran share some great stories and incidents in their lives and how each of them dealt with similar situations focusing on the life lessons. The Ramcharran's provide a guide to show readers how to use these 11 Life Lessons to break limitations, discover the true you, and how to build a framework needed to achieve goals and to build quality relationship with you loved ones. The 11 life lessons are a symbol of life situations that can be utilized by all, old and young to help guide maturity.

Malhar & Dr. Ram P. Ramcharran

Malhar's New

Chapter 1

There is no such thing as cannot.

I am always on edge about drawing and making artwork. But that wasn't always the case when I was a kid. I would only draw in little snippets in my free time, I had when I was younger. I showed my old art pieces to my mom and dad and they said they liked them. Unfortunately, I did not get the same reaction from my art teacher at the time. She pointed out certain flaws in my pieces, like the arms, legs,

and eyes being crooked or the perspective being confusing to perceive. I was pretty devastated that I wasn't meeting the standards of someone who I thought was a professional at the time. I was starting to lose confidence in my skills as an artist since I wasn't getting the results that I needed. Fortunately, my parents stopped me from giving up on my art. They told me that I was still learning a new skill and I shouldn't get so worked up over my first attempts. I just needed more time to study art and develop my talents; after that, I would be able to produce far more satisfying work.. I didn't give up; I was able to learn the more basic and advanced attributes for drawing with how well I've gotten at this type of training and the hard work I've put in over the last few years, I feel I am on my way to becoming a much better artist and ultimately an animator, and I really hope to expand it in my future career. I started to notice things that contribute to structure and perspective in my drawings, and the character development I created was taking form. Like my parents said, "There is no such thing as cannot" as long you work towards your goals.

LESSON ONE

"There is no such thing as cannot"

"Sooner or later, those who win are those who think they can"– By Richard Bach

Malhar's experience with "There is no such thing as cannot"

My dad always wanted me to swim with him during the summer months, but I kept saying I can't do it! My dad and old brother Rohan would be in the pool for hours just having fun. "I will never be able to swim" I kept saying to him. For years my parents had me in swimming lessons, from as early as age 3. I was in swim seals, the YMCA and for two summers I had swimming coaches come to my house giving me private lessons in my own pool. Until they enrolled me in summer camp at countryside country club where they had a super swim team. That swim coach was one of the counselors during my time at the club. During the swimming activities, I learned how to tread water, gain speed and do other various swimming strokes. I then became faster than my own family. It wasn't until one day my dad insisted that I come swimming with him and my brother that he tossed me in the pool where suddenly, I was swimming in front of my family. It was the most awesome feeling. The lesson here was my dad never gave up on me and did many things to help me learn and accomplish what I thought at the time would be impossible. He was correct when is said "there is no such thing as cannot." Thanks Dad!

CHAPTER 1

∞∞∞∞∞∞∞∞∞∞∞∞∞∞∞∞∞

There is no such thing as cannot

I always remember my dad's words "There is no such thing is can't" and the same way my dad would enthusiastically tell me there is no such thing as can't I find myself continuously saying the same thing to Malhar and to myself. As I have gotten older and I believe somewhat wiser or I guess had more life experience, I find that if I use good old common sense I am able to make the right decisions when it at times it seems impossible on what direction to go or what choice to make. What I know for certain is there is definitely no such thing as can't Most recently, whenever I wanted to give up on this new formulation that I had been working on for more than a year, I never seemed to do so because I could hear in the back of my head that there is no such thing as can't. Those words from my father always seemed to come back to me when I wanted to give up and walk away from this goal. It is like a cheerleader in your head that keeps pushing you forward telling you not to give up and to continue to try new things and to do things outside the box and to find new ways to be innovative I remember being on the verge of throwing in the towel when I had a breakthrough that completely altered the outcomes of the non-alcoholic formulations I had been working on for more than a year and a half. Suddenly, it came to me that if I added just one more ingredient, it would bring together all of the components and make them balanced, flavorful, aromatic, and most importantly, give them a mouth-watering sensation like it was the real thing.. As crazy as it may have seemed to add this one unique item, it actually worked. However, there was now a need to find a way to protect the process and formulation, so I was thrilled when my attorney suggested creating my creations under a trade secret like Kentucky Fried Chicken, CocaCola, and Krispy Kreme Donuts. The lesson here is simple if you can remember when things seem impossible and lost you can rely on these simple words to keep you going "there is no such thing as can't" and you find a way to overcome.

Dad's experience

You are eight years old and you have been tasked to go find a screw driver in your father's tool box in the outside tool shed. It's cold dark and wet outside where the detached garage was located, you make your way across the drive way in the freezing slushy cold and nasty snow to rummage through your father's tool box to find a star point (Philips screwdriver) as my father would call it. Once you get there you are totally lost and for one you are scared out of your mind and to add to that it is totally dark, and you can't find the pull string light switch and you are hearing squeaking sounds in the dark making you more and more scared to move forward to find the screwdriver that your father so adamantly demanded. You make some feeble attempts to look for it in the dark so what do you? You run, screaming you saw a rat staring at you while you were attempting to turn on the light. True or not that's what just happened and then to return to your dad telling him you can't find the screwdriver that he so adamantly demanded of you. So, what next, I go and tell my dad there's no screwdriver in the shed, just from seeing his expression I will never forget because he specifically told me where to go and where to look however, due to my inability at the time to see past my nervousness I had to return and tell him there is no screw driver– at the time I can't remember what was scary seeing my father's demeanor that I didn't listen to him or the idea of running into a rat in the shed. Nonetheless my dad being the patient gentlemen that he was, he did not prove me wrong, he said let's go find it together. I grabbed his fat fingers over his gloves and proceeded to the shed knowing I was afraid only to find within two minutes of the walk from the garage to the shed my dad turned the light switch on and opened the tool box, turning to me presenting the star point screw driver just simply saying to me son, "there is no such thing as cannot" all you had to was follow my directions and you would have gotten the task done. Now looking back all these years later I wish I had opened my mouth and told my dad I was really scared of the dark and I thought I saw a rat's eyes staring at me hence I ran away, and I thought he would have had a point on that as well, but I never told him so instead I learned a lesson. It probably tells Malhar, me or whoever you work for that you're not giving any effort, or you just want to give up.

Chapter 2

Why wait? Don't Procrastinate.

When I was in the fifth grade, I had to do an egg drop project. It was more or less just a simple way to test if an egg will survive being dropped in your little container or not. Me being young, thought it would be as simple as it could get to drop it, record the results, and that would be the end of it.. I didn't realize this wouldn't be an easy task until I realized I had to write out each thought and step of the constructing process in addition to responding

 to a few questions. I, on the other hand, was too busy with other things to pay attention and work on it. As a result, I did not receive the high grade I wanted.. My parents were on edge about me wasting time for something as small as this. I wouldn't have to spend extra time making up the assignment if I had just thought about how I would record and write for my project. The lesson of Why wait? Don't procrastinate was once again proven by the result I received by not being proactive with the task at hand.

LESSON TWO

~~~~~~~~~~~~~~~~~~~~~~

"Why Wait?" Don't Procrastinate

"You may delay, but time will not"– Benjamin Franklin

Malhar's experience with "Why Wait?"

When I was in the second grade I had to do a volcano project for school for Mrs. Flannigan class. She said to make a fan made volcano. But when I had to do it I didn't sweat it because it was easy. She then changed it to a real volcano that would work. That's when I finished my fan made one and didn't do anything all week. My dad told me I could make some improvements to the volcano, but I said I didn't have to. Then I found out on the day it had to be turned in, it was changed to a real volcano. So, I ended up getting an F on the project. The lesson here was that if I had completed the volcano earlier and when I found out about the new changes I had ample time to fix it or at least could have tried to get it completed and up to the new standard that was given. I learned a hard lesson on this "Why wait?" life lesson that my dad would drum into my ears especially when it came to my school work and chores at home. My dad always tried to put me in a situation to be successful and by adopting this lesson you too can learn ways to make yourself better.

CHAPTER 2

Why wait? Don't Procrastinate

I was in a funk after the passing of one my favorite uncles. I was very close to him and he was a wonderful and caring gentlemen, he would give you the shirt of his back and was always there to help anyone in need. I was not dealing well how he died. He was helping a neighbor cut some branches on his trees in their front yard and in a split second he fell off the ladder and hit head on the ground and never woke back up. He was in a coma for almost three weeks despite all the prayers and medical attention he received there was nothing they could do to bring him back eventually our family had to take him off life support. It was a tough way to see him his last days. He was a man's man. He cared for his family, brother, sisters and friends and to see him pass this way was extremely hard for me to deal with this especially after we just had met a few weeks earlier while he was visiting my mom in the hospital after she had surgery. That was an eye-opening experience for him to see his younger sister in the hospital and he felt he needed to start living his life and enjoy the fruits of his labor. We had a lengthy and detailed chat that day and he promised to stop postponing his vacations and doing things with family and community service and he was going on his first vacation in over 5 years next month. He was so happy that day and smiling and laughing and telling stories of how he overcame his fears and how to be a better person. My uncle told me that he should never have put off doing the things he needed to do and that he should find more time to enjoy everything he had worked so hard to achieve. He also stated that seeing my mother in the hospital had given him the push he needed to start living his life, and he was going to do so right away.. This is a clear example that we should not put things off for tomorrow when we can do it today or in the immediate future especially if it would be beneficial to you and your loved ones. Why wait? Don't procrastinate is a lesson that I learned from this experience with my uncle. I continue to try to be proactive in my life and not put off now things I can do vs tomorrow.

Dad's experience:

I can vividly remember when I was in the 8th grade– Middle school, I was tasked over the semester to make a functioning scale model of a garage and bring it to science class and demonstrate it in front of my science teacher and the rest of the class. I had over two and a half months to prepare and plan for this project. My dad would constantly ask how the progress was coming on the garage and I would say it's coming, I am working on the design and the layout. As an eighth grader, I was a pretty shy person and was not really looking forward to getting in front of the class to talk about the project. I knew what I was making and how to go about it but the thought of having to explain in front of a group terrified me to the point I just kept putting the project off until I had 3 days left. I finally went to my dad for help, so I wouldn't get a failing grade. It was a difficult conversation because I kept telling him I was working on it and that I was almost done but the truth was I was done in my head not on building out the project. When I finally asked for help and confessed why I was waiting to do the actual building, I felt very silly because dad was direct and straight "Why wait?" he said again he turned to me and said you could have built this project early and spend the rest of the time practicing on the things that made you feel uneasy, so you could become super prepare for the demonstration. He knew I could design the project and how to put it together relatively quickly, but he was now concerned I would be so stressed out about the presentation which was more than 70% of the grade, instead I spent no time preparing because I was so far behind in getting the project complete. What ultimately happened was I was able to assemble the project and practice with my dad for the presentation which I got an A on, but I wasted so much valued time by not being proactive on building and learning how to make a proper presentation. The lesson of "Why wait?" stays with me each and every day. I have learned to do today instead of tomorrow because I am only losing valuable time and creating more effort when it's not necessary. You're probably hoping for your parent to give you something for when you finished a chore, but they tell you it must be done before they get home from work, or you don't get your reward. But you start wasting time and when they get home you don't get your reward.

Chapter 3

Don't wait till you have to poop to build the toilet.

My final year of elementary school was treated as if it were my first year of middle school, and it certainly seemed that way. I was a pretty nervous wreck starting off, and unfortunately it projected a little into my performance in certain subjects. Being in a new place, having a new schedule, and meeting new people like staff and students made the fifth grade an emotional roller coaster for me. Since I was so preoccupied with trying to "collect" myself, when in reality I was just using dopamine as a tool to combat it through books, movies, and games, I kind of panicked about getting things done since I kept on waiting till the last minute.. Mom and Dad saw through all of my attempts to extend my time to myself, calling it unhealthy for my health, habits, and future. They told me I had to stop

just turning my hobbies into dopamine factories just to make myself feel slightly better and instead start working on myself in my new middle school environment. I made the decision to quit bringing myself down and to start reconnecting with some old friends. Soon we were warming up again, and I was making new friends with some of my new peers that my friends had gotten to know. I was still a bit shy but I was pretty good through middle school, not perfect, but good to actually go and enjoy it instead of waiting until the last few easy days or weeks we had to try and bond In order to be proactive in my new environment, I had to make use of all the abilities, resources, and knowledge I already had. As expected the lessons, I was given ahead of time proved to be useful.

LESSON THREE

"Don't wait till you have to poop before you build the toilet"- Don't wait till the last minute

"All our dreams can come true if we have the courage to purse them"

Walt Disney

Malhar's experience of waiting for the last minute:

When I was in the second grade, I had a cloud project which was about the weather patterns and what it looked like during the week. This project required to work on every day in order to gather all the necessary information to complete the assignment for my class project which was more than half of my projects grade. The project required me recording the cloud patterns every day from Monday to Friday and the weather. I was given three weeks to complete the project I had to pick one week over that three weeks period to use. Unfortunately, I decided to wait until the last week of the 3 given and on the next Monday it was due, then I needed to make a presentation of what happened through those 5 days. But as faith would have it I got sick for most of that week and I was not really able to focus on the project like I needed to, so I didn't do it one bit of it because I thought I could finish it later when I felt better. This forced me to work on it all day on Sunday which was the one day my parents would allow me to play my electronic games. It made it so difficult because I had to go back and research what the weather was for the week and sometimes had to guess what the weather was like as well. I was still feeling sick, so I didn't finish it all the way like I wanted to. I presented it on Monday and it didn't go as well as I liked. A week later I got back my grade lucky enough to get 70% a C-. Ever since that experience, I always try to make sure that every piece of my homework and projects are done before I do anything else. This experience taught me a lot other than just trying to get my homework and school projects done on time. It taught me to be more proactive in whatever I do and to try to be more in tuned and not be a procrastinator in trying to accomplish my task at hand.

CHAPTER 3

Don't wait till you have to poop to build the toilet

This is saying is one that I really can appreciate as a grown up and most importantly as a professional in the business and medical field. Don't wait till you have to poop to build the toilet. Simple translation is, do not wait till the last-minute to do something you are required to do. Being proactive is a really good quality and trait to have, and it's important to embrace and most important to embrace because this is all within your own power. When you can control the process and when you control the process that means you should have a good idea of what the outcome will be. . As I sit down to write this update of what Malhar and I have been doing over the last four years as we have both grown as individuals and as a family and as our relationship as father and son has grown. I realize that I have a son who is so proactive that at times I find myself telling him to please slow down and spend some time enjoying this summer of 2023 with your friends and do some fun things because your youth will be over before you know it. His response was Dad I have to concentrate on my career. At first I was like what career, I want him to enjoy his time off and he is looking out for the future at the ripe old age of 17. He is starting his senior year this year and already knows what career he wants to pursue and what he wants to do for the rest of his adult life for work. He has embraced his passion and talent in art and computers and has been proactively working on his own animated characters with story lines so he can prepare for early entrance and acceptance into the university of choice.. No matter which one he decides to attend, he will not wait until the last minute to apply to colleges or other institutions. Because he already knows what he wants to do, I find myself pushing him to apply to as many places that have programs that are applicable to his desires for furthering his postsecondary education. Malhar and I have both embraced this Ramcharran family rule to be proactive I really believe that we have a far better chance of success in everything we do if we wait to take the appropriate actions and control the situation on our own terms. If we take the initiative, we won't have to worry or rush to play catchup. I am sure everyone who is reading this passage at this moment can immediately think of a situation where they waited to build the toilet before they needed to poop (LOL).

Dad's experience:

This is a statement my mom and dad use to tell me a lot since I was such a proactive person when I was growing up, whenever I would hear them say this to me I knew for sure I messed up and there was going to be a follow up lesson for my lack of awareness. I remember when I was seventeen years old, dad told me when I got my first car I would be responsible for maintaining and paying for my car insurance and I promised that I would make sure I take care of it since I was working on the weekends. I prided myself at an early age to be proactive and responsible for my own duties however; apparently, I was distracted enough that I didn't, I would drive my car at times and on a couple of occasions I actually ran out of gas while driving. I had this very bad habit of waiting for the very last minute to fill gas in the tank that it turned out to be disastrous for me because I got stuck on the side of the road more than once which was embarrassing and dangerous. I did wait for the last-minute lots of times and it didn't work out so well for me. I should know not to wait especially with something as important as that. I actually ran out of gas a quarter mile away from my house and believe me it was horrible because I knew what my dad was going to say to me and it was not good to hear because I knew he was right and the last thing I wanted to hear was "Don't wait till you have to poop before you build the toilet; don't wait till the last minute, how many times do I have to remind you of that son." The second time I ran of gas I was about 35 miles away visiting some friends and it was late at night. I kept saying I will stop soon to fill up gas I have some time then all of a sudden when I was ready to stop and fill up my tank there was no place to stop and I kept driving and driving thinking I would find a gas station. Back in the day when I was growing up they didn't have internet or apps to help you find a filling station close by you, you had to know where you were going and what was around you. All of a sudden, I am on the highway and my car starts to sputter and choke as it was running out of gas, finally I am forced to come to a full stop in the late evening in the dark. Luckily, I was close to an exit that I only had to walk a few miles to get to a phone to call my dad to come get me and to again hear how many times I have to tell you young man, "Don't wait till you have to poop before you build the toilet" I just stood there and took it like a man because he was absolutely correct again. If you do wait till the last minute you could miss out on something you like or fail a school project or an assignment.

Chapter 4

~~~~~~~~~~~~~~

Don't be a follower, be the leader.

As I continue to grow up, I sometimes feel my father always questions me on if I'll be a leader or a follower. It was just like how Grandpa would ask the same question to him over and over again I was told. As much as I sometimes hesitate about it, I like to think I was naturally born to be a leader. When I was a child, I told my father that I would rather be a leader than a follower, mainly because I did not like to take constant orders. I

eventually settles down on not following orders and instead translated it more as listening. This is because, while a follower does pay attention to what a leader says, a leader also listens to his or her followers to gather information about those followers or to determine what needs to be done. In my sophomore year of high school, I was assigned to make a slideshow about the history of the Chinese dynasties as a four-person-group project with a couple people I was not very familiar with but with one friend who I was familiar with them. We had a bit of a rocky start since no one could agree on what should be what or who should do what. I was feeling a bit overwhelmed because no one could settle on one idea for the project. I decided to try and step up much to the dismay of a couple protesters and set things right for us. I apologized for silencing everyone but I informed them that we had to work together on this project if we want to get through it with an excellent grade. I asked everyone what their strong points were and we laid out a plan. Someone would do research on each of the dynasties, someone would write about each of them, someone would refine the info and polish it up to make it look good, and someone would help lead the presentation for the end of the project. Thanks to our teamwork we got an A on the assignment. I learned the importance of how me taking charge and leading also required me to listen to those I was trying to lead. I learned that a good leader does what is right for their followers no matter what and tries to lift their mood without just pandering to them or being overly judgmental.

LESSON FOUR

~~~~~~~~~~~~~~~~~~~~~~~~~~~~~~~~

"Be a leader not a follower" You make the choice that's best for you!

"The only safe ship in a storm is leadership"– Faye Wattleton

Malhar's experience as a leader:

My dad was always all over me when it came to this question of being a leader or a follower. Ever since I could remember my Dad shared the story of what I am going to choose to be– a follower or a leader. He told me over and over what my grandpa's use to ask him and tell him to choose. As long as I could remember the Ramcharran's rule were buried into my head. Dad would say your grandpas would tell me the same thing over and over and now it is his turn to ask me the same question. I think I was born a natural leader so when he asked me what do I want to be a leader or a follower–I started giggling because I didn't like to take orders, I wanted to be in charge to a point that it got me in trouble a lot at school, I was telling the other kids in my class what to do even when I was not in a position to do so. It came easy for me to be proactive in anything I did. For example, I knew I was a leader when I first entered kindergarten. When my teacher Mrs. Hoffer was out sick, I would go to the substitute teacher and offer my help to share what we were doing in the class without being asked and wanted to help with managing the kids in the class especially when the kids would get rowdy and out of control with talking and messing around. I would offer to help, and I would start telling the other kids to behave and not make noise or to not misbehave when the substitute teacher was trying to tell the class what to do. On one occasion, one of the students started running on the way to the lunch room so I told the others in my class to stop miss behaving and follow directions just as if our teacher Mrs. Hoffer was here telling us what to do. I quickly realized that it came naturally to want to be in the lead and to help make things happen; however, how small or large it was. I will tell you with certainty I got in trouble many times for wanting to help but I know it was something I wanted to do to be in front. I never wanted to be a show off, but I wanted to be helpful in everything I did. I think If you want to be a leader you should take pride and learn what it is to be a leader at the same time as I have learned from dad saying great leaders are also excellent followers as well when they are not leading they take that time to learn how to be better when in charge. If you lie instead of fessing up and telling the truth, it will get you in even more trouble.

CHAPTER 4

Don't be a follower, be the leader

In this example that I'm going to give you is all about being a leader and not a follower. In the last few years, I have transitioned from working in medicine to working in more of a business environment. I had come to the realization that I enjoyed working with my wife in the medical field but when she passed away from cancer that joy also went away. Seeing patients and helping people was a joy we shared and when that wasn't possible any longer I had to reassess my life and how I was going to move forward. One of the things we both enjoyed was business and building things. The last few years before she passed away we had identified a market segment that we believe could be the next revolution in helping people and at the same time change the beverage market space by creating functional beverages that would make people feel better and have experiences that help their body and mind. In 2020 during the COVID pandemic we decided that we would spend our time learning and formulating ingredients that would make a difference. Between her treatment and downtime, we committed all of our free time to developing formulas and flavor profiles that we thought the general public would enjoy in order to work toward becoming the industry leader rather than waiting for someone else to develop and own the space. After Malhar's mom lost her battle with cancer, I continued to work towards this goal to become the best in this space and to work tireless till I perfect formulations that are accepted in the market space. I am happy to say after 3 years we were able to launch 7 different nonalcoholic beverages that are unique and one of a kind in the market space that has gained traction and market share.

Dad's experience:

Ever since I was a little boy my dad and uncle use to tell me there are only two types of people in this world leaders or followers, which one are you going to choose to be? They used to tell me this over and over again every time I had a decision to make. When I was little, I did not really understand what they meant but as I got an older, I firmly started to get what they meant and what they were trying to tell me about life. When I was around 10 or 11 It just came to me that I wanted to be a leader not a follower. I realized that being a follower was a lot easier to me. All I had to do was wait for things to happen and wait for someone to tell me what I needed to do. I quickly decided that was boring and not for me.

It all started for me when I decided to take control of how I was going to do my chores around the house. Instead of waiting for my parents to tell me daily I needed to take out the garbage or wash the cars I would take the initiative and do them without having to be told what to do. I quickly realized that my parents were less restrictive with me when I wanted to go out and play with my friends or go out and ride my bike in the neighborhood it was always yes. It became apparent quickly they started trusting me more and when I asked for things they didn't hesitate to say yes to me. I know my initiative of being more proactive with my chores and task led them to being more open and free to let me do more things I wanted to do with my friends or have more freedom to make my own choices or decision even how small they were at the time. It was an amazing feeling to be able to take charge and to be proactive and outgoing with my decisions. Being a leader didn't always go as I planned but it was way more fun and rewarding in the end. Make the choice to lead not follow you will be better off for it. If you ever want to be big, great and famous, you first have to learn how to be a leader because if you're just a follower you'll be getting halfway results or probably nothing.

Chapter 5

~~~~~~~~~~~~~~~~~~~~~~

Always take responsibility for your own actions& mistakes.

No matter how much time passes, along with the many other Ramcharran's rules, I always remember to take responsibility for your own actions and tell the truth, no matter how bad it may hurt; I was told to confess, come clean, and make sure to tell the truth and take responsibility for my own actions. A lot of these times mostly applied to my school life, but it especially applied to my everyday life. My parents always emphasized how important this characteristic is for me to have. I also wanted this for myself as I know it is the morally correct thing to do.. However, just like everyone in the world, I did not always tell the whole truth or give the whole story. I would sometimes lie to my teachers on occasions when I did something wrong because I did not want to get in trouble. And when they did know I did something wrong or eventually found out, they would make me tell my parents. When telling my parents, I would lie to them as well. I would either withhold some of the information or not tell them the entire situation because I was scared of the consequences. I did not want to be grounded or to feel ostracized. It started out as I was in my middle school science class, reading the class textbook, instead of paying attention to the slideshow lesson. At the time I was tuning out the lesson because I felt confident

that I had already gotten most of the information for the current chapter and was more or less thinking about working ahead. This happened for about a week and my science teacher was not having it. On the first Monday, he told me to pay attention and put the textbook down. I rubbed it off like it was nothing, saying, "alright I will", but my bookworm instincts took over and I went back to reading instead of paying attention like I should have been. As the first week progressed, I was continuously called out and continued to lie about paying attention. I ended up not doing as well as I wanted to on the first the exam day. Since I got a low score on the test, I panicked and told my parents that it was probably just a mistake on the teacher's behalf, or I could just make it up later once I could. What I did not know was that my parents received an email from my science teacher about me not paying attention in class and focusing on working ahead in the textbook. I was confronted by my parents and was grounded for lying to them and my science teacher. Fortunately, I got to retake my assessment and passed with flying colors after apologizing. It wasn't the first time I messed up by lying out of fear, I lied about giving a great effort when I was younger and on the swim team even though It felt like I was just killing time I suppose. Though I use to do whatever I can to avoid getting in trouble. I now know I deserved to get in trouble at the times I did. I am now going into my senior year of high school; this August 2023 know it is best to always take responsibility for my actions no matter what. making it my duty to always try to tell the truth and take responsibility so I can be the person I need to be and want to be.

LESSON FIVE

~~~~~~~~~~~~~~~~~~~~~~~~~~~

Always take responsibility for your own actions and mistakes

"The price of greatness is responsibility"– Winston Churchill

Malhar's experience

Ever since I could remember one of the Ramcharran's rules of the house has always been, take responsibility for your actions and tell the truth even if it hurts. I was told to make sure to tell the truth and take responsibility for my own actions a lot of times especially when it came to school and life by my mom and dad. They always felt that was an important characteristic for me to have and I wanted to do that as well for me because I knew it was the right thing to do. However, I did not always tell the whole truth or give the whole story, I lied to my teachers on occasions when I did something wrong because I did not want to get in trouble. And when they did know I did something wrong, they made me tell my parents, but I still lied to my parents, by either withholding info or not telling them the entire situation because I was scared of getting grounded. However, my teachers somehow figured out that I was not telling the truth to my parents; So, they started to email them every single thing that happened whenever I did not speak up right away. When I was caught doing something bad or something wrong they sent it by email. My teachers typed up everything I did like It was being stalked or having a rumor spread or a bunch of gossip it felt like. I found out by my parents as soon I was picked up from school. Every time I was getting into trouble; my teachers would inform my parents by emailing them on the computer. Well I did not, and I mean NOT expect getting my stuff taken away for a punishment instead of getting pounded (Not intentionally) or a big talk or discussion. So, while I was restricted I was sulking until it was all over. But this was not the first time I lied and did not take responsibilities. When I lied about turning in or doing classwork or homework, I deserved to get in trouble. Sometimes I think I was lucky I was not held back or sent back a grade because I use to mess around a lot when I go back and think about it as I am now in middle school. But It wasn't the end of it. I even lied about giving a great effort on the swim team even though I was just killing time I suppose. So, from now on I always tell the truth and take responsibilities.

CHAPTER 5

~~~~~~~~~~~~~~~~~

Always take responsibility for your
own actions & mistakes

If you want to give your life true meaning and purpose, I think that everyone who wants to be a good citizen should embrace the idea of accepting responsibility for your own acts and mistakes. You see, when you use excuses and avoid taking responsibility, you eventually have a feeling of emptiness in your life because you are not being honest with yourself. I recently made the mistake of investing in a new business venture when I thought I had done all the necessary research and due diligence before signing on to become a partner in a pharmaceutical company that my advisor thought would be a great addition to our portfolio of business entities and at the same time would be the perfect fit to help manufacture the new beverages we were developing and launching. The problem is I made a serious mistake in making this investment and it has cost me dearly because I vetted the business and the building, but I totally missed what turned out to be the most important aspect of this investment and partnership that was the majority shareholder. I never took the time to research him and understand why his company was in the state it was in and why he desperately needed a partner to save his business. I made a crave mistake by not learning about him, his actions, his behavior and why he treats people like he does and never takes responsibility for the state the company was in. I didn't want to accept that I made a mistake by ignoring the behavior and actions how he treated his staff and people in the company. Due to our failure to properly understand and participate in the process, this mistake and oversight caused a significant setback for our company and raised concerns about the viability of the company as a whole. Like anything else, once I admitted I made a major mistake and admitted and took personal responsibility for this blunder I was able to ask for help from my other partners to help find a way to put a plan together to fix this problem. I am happy to report after speaking with some professionals and getting help with this problem we are on our way to fixing this matter.

Dad's experience:

This is a very important lesson for me to share with you. As I was growing up as a little boy my dad pounded this rule into me just like I do now to my son. I can remember one time it was my turn to help clean out the storage room at my dad's grocery store in Bronx, NY where I grew up. It was an unwritten duty that was assigned to me, my brother and sister at the time. We were to take turns to clean out the storage room monthly so when the new supplies arrived it was nice and neat, and the delivery would be placed in the right sections and be able to be distributed easily throughout the store. For a few weeks I was able to have my little brother fill in for me and then I had my sister take my turn as well. All the time, my dad was under the impression I was doing my share of the work and handling my responsibility but I wasn't and I started lacking in my duties and was taking advantage of my siblings because on the Saturdays when it was my turn to clean out the storage room I was too interested in going to the movies downtown with my friends than doing my work and taking responsibilities of task assigned to me. My dad finally came to me one day. If you lie instead of fessing up and telling the truth, it will get you in even more trouble.

Chapter 6

Don't live your life looking through the rear-view mirror.

A big part of my life I fear the most is past mistakes and sins. Not just for my own image but also those I hold close to my heart. This is because of how I might represent their influence on me and how I view them. But what tugs on the back of my mind is the people I feel I have wronged or hurt ESPECIALLY my loved ones. I know the saying about karma and how it affects people from good and bad actions determining the respective results by putting them on their conscience. Personally, I continue to fear my accidents may also translate as a bad omen on my karma. I have always dwelled on everyone I felt I have hurt or didn't do good enough for them. I am now learning to be better at looking ahead not backwards. After my mother got cancer, I felt scared and upset that I couldn't do anything to support her. However, my family convinced me to be strong and confident for her sake and my own because that is what she would have wanted for the both of us. Fortunately for her and family, my mother had overcome cancer and was doing great. I was glad that she was finally coming back to being her old beautiful and lively self. But, the worst was yet to come. Over the next few months, COVID-19 was still happening, and we soon were required to get vaccinated. Soon, my mom started having some liver issues due to the vaccine. So, my father and her went on a long journey on the road all over the country to find treatments to help her get better. After returning home with little success, which was a traumatic experience; she ended up having a seizure that was caused by the vaccine.. She was rushed to the hospital and had to stay there in a coma to recover. Unfortunately, she didn't make it through. I was taken out of school to say my final goodbyes to her before having to watch them unplug my mother's life support. It was the most horrible and hurtful time in my life. This is an experience I don't wish anyone should have to go through.. Soon a funeral was held where everyone who knew her came up to say their goodbyes. People went up to the podium to deliver speeches on what happened through my mother's wonderful but cut-short life. My father also went up to the podium to say a few words. I stood beside him, but I remained silent. We all cried and grieved over her unfortunate passing. But soon I started to develop guilt and regret. I went to my mother's funeral but didn't say anything. Thoughts like, "Why didn't I?!" and "I should've!", echoed through my head. I felt like I refused to say something at the funeral because I just wanted to keep it to myself or no one would understand. But it would've been good for me to give a funeral speech so people could try and sympathize or empathize with me is how I felt. If not both or either. I simply felt that I had to keep quiet about something that should have been cleared up on my conscience. I was soon approached by my father and grandfather after trying to avoid confrontation until it became inevitable. They told me that my feeling of guilt and regret of not speaking my emotions is understandable but the length I had it going on for was unnecessary. I had come clean with myself about what I felt was a mistake. They told me not to feel guilty because they acknowledged that I was emotional and feeling as if I was in a very tight spot to speak. At my mother's funeral, I had the opportunity to speak, but I chose not to because I didn't know what to say or simply couldn't do so due to my mental state. Looking back, I realize it was normal for me to feel the way I did at the time. I never tried to keep secrets from my mother, so I had nothing to worry about. I now know from this experience what I should have been doing is keeping my head up and pressing on through life because that's what she would have wanted. I soon stopped looking behind me and drowning myself in pity and sorrow and started to look to my future with my family and focused on the memories she gave me while she was here and celebrating her legacy. My mom was an incredible lady, she was an amazing physician, community leader, businesswoman and most of all the best mom anyone could hope for and for that I am looking forward not backwards.

LESSON SIX

"Don't live your life looking through the rear-view mirror"

So, we beat on the boats against the current, borne back ceaselessly into the past"– F. Scott Fitzgerald

Malhar's Experience:

When I was about 3 my dad had me go out and try to swim with him. Well, I was freaked out when I saw the pool. It was deep, but I didn't know how deep it was. I went in but I fell deep and couldn't swim up. My father had to rescue me from the pool and dry me off. 2 years later, he had me try and swim again. I was freaked out when we were about to do that. I told Dad that I wasn't going to make it out of the pool alive and I might sink like last time. But Dad said I shouldn't look back to the past. I asked him why and he said "The rear-view mirror doesn't matter. What matters is what happens when you take risks and try to do something you think you can or can't do." That's how I ended up learning how to swim like a professional after I learned how to swim with my father and finished the seasons when I joined the swim team. So, to this day I've learned how the past doesn't matter. I didn't only learn this from my father, I also learned it from a rich and famous man named Warren Buffet. He is famous for giving business advice. But he also taught about the rear-view mirror. His speech about it goes something like this: "The rear-view mirror is always clearer then the windshield. If you don't have a clear picture of where you want to go, you can get into trouble. Paying attention to where you've been, gives you a clear picture of where to go." I've always dreamed of being successful and talked to everyone I knew for answers. Although I did make mistakes I was able to get through. "Remember, see your future, be your future." When I heard that speech I knew for sure that I should never pay attention to the past all the way to this day.

CHAPTER 6

~~~~~~~~~~~~~~~~~~~~~~~~~~

Don't live your life looking through the rear-view mirror!

This is one of my favorite sayings that my dad used to say to us over and over. He used to preach this rule to my sibling's when we were growing up. The same thing seems to happen as I am raising my children as well. I find myself telling them if you are looking backwards, you can't see the opportunity Iinfront of you. It took a while for me to really understand what he was trying to say to us and what it really meant to be able to shrug off tragedy, setback, failure, and even hurt feelings. It's natural for people to want to spend time playing in their head their mistakes or heartbreak trying to figure why it happened or how they could have prevented it. What I've learned as I've gotten older and gained more life experience is that it doesn't really matter why things happen or how they happen; what matters more is that we figure out how to deal with the occurrence and how to move on without squandering energy on things we can't control. A great example of "Don't live your life looking through the rear-view mirror" is when Malhar's mom passed away, I spent hours and hours, days and nights trying to figure out what I could have done differently to get her better treatment and what we could have done to prevent the cancer that consumed her.. Malhar still needed my attention and focus because he was so young and in need of it, and I was missing out on seeing his needs and missing out on comforting him more during the pain we were experiencing as I couldn't get rid of the feeling that I hadn't done enough to help save. While doing this, it consumed every moment of my life. I had to remind myself we still have some much more to live for and that there is so much to do and grow as a dad, a man and as a person. I could not see this because I was spending all my time feeling sorry for myself and that not seeing what was important to me and that was Malhar and my other children and family. I was looking through the rearview mirror and spending so much time in the past that I couldn't see what the future might hold, and, most importantly, not spending any time with Malhar, who needed me the most. I finally understood that Malhar need my attention and that there was still so much to look forward to. I'll remind everyone that when you experience pain and loss , it's not the end of the world— just remember the good times you've had and what's to come when you see the light ahead.

Dad's experience:

Don't live your life looking through the rear-view mirror was always a difficult one for me to understand while growing up. My dad was always saying that to me because I would dwell on things that already happened, and I would get frustrated trying to think how I could have handled things better. It was tough for me to until one day it suddenly came to me what he was saying, it was like a light went off in my head. I remember vividly when I took the law school exam and I got the results back and I did not do as well as I should have to get into the schools I was applying for. I was frustrated and upset that my scores were just okay. They were acceptable, but I felt I could have done better and I was sulking for almost a month and kept saying how could this happen to me after studying so much on my own and I was dedicated to the process of getting into school. My dad came to me one afternoon after hearing me tell my mom that I worked hard, and I know I should have gotten a better score on the test. Dad said why are you looking back instead of concentrating on the future. He said if you want to get into the schools you are applying to you need to go seek help and study properly for the exam. He said, "it's only a setback not the end of the world son." After hearing that the next day I went to Kaplan learning training center and signed up for the LSAT exam training class, so I could learn the proper tools of taking test. It was an intense 6 weeks class that I had to take in the evenings which was very inconvenient for me since I was working and going to school at the time. I realize that if I did not take control of my emotions and feeling about not doing well on the exam it was going to consume me. I am happy to say after taking the course I did very well on the exam when I took it again and I applied to my choices of schools getting into the one I wanted. I was very happy that my dad had that conversation with me and from time on I took the lesson to heart, whereas now I am sharing that same message to my sons.

Chapter 7

~~~~~~~~~~~~~~~

You have to be your own man in life.

Growing up, I was always reluctant to stand up for myself, never really speaking out against people trying to put me down. It was more or less out of fear of people perceiving it the wrong way or getting in trouble for being misjudged. It unfortunately made me look even weaker than I already was feeling. I was an easy target to manipulate, being very quiet with low confidence at times. I was also unfortunately unable to learn how to tune out and ignore people I didn't like that was mean to me. So, I would reach the point of feeling as if I was going mad over

people's bullying. I eventually went to my dad during my blood boiling middle school years to complain about my school life. He understood my frustrations but emphasized that I should try working on myself instead of worrying what others may think or do to me and how I should not let them get into my head. After hearing my dad out, I have felt pretty strong despite my looks of being tall and skinny with sticks for arms. After sharing the experience with my dad and listening to the things I am good at and things that make me special in my own way, I feel like I'm in control of who I am now; No one can try to boss me around or try to tell me otherwise when it comes to things that I know are proper and correct, but never to the point where I'm selfishly absorbed. Today I feel that I can be my own man in life and take a stance when others are trying to bully or push me to do things I am not comfortable with.

LESSON SEVEN

"Always be your own man"

"Always be a first-rate version of yourself and not a second-rate version of someone else"– Judy Garland

Malhar's Experience

I used to be a bit of a coward and not standup for myself and just take the abuse. I never let my instincts kick in to standup. So, I complained to my father and then he told me that the reason I was getting bothered was because I wasn't being tough enough and was making myself look weak. So, after he told me that I then stood up to everyone who put me down and told them I'm my own man and if you want to be a man you got to make sure you toughen up. Even though it did help sometimes it sort of got me in bad situations. But that's how I became my own man. Before I even complained to Dad, I was stuck in kindergarten with some rude and annoying boy named Lukas. This boy constantly bothered me. But when it came to my birthday, he literally made me get in trouble for no reason. It was just a misunderstood joke with his name in it. When I got in trouble he screamed, "YES!!!!!!!!." I'd say kindergarten was the worst year of my life because of my teacher Ms. Hofer. After that long year of pain, I would have called her Ms. Horrid because she was not a good teacher in my opinion who I believed really cared about her students.

CHAPTER 7

You have to be your own man in life

You have to be your own man in life is so very true. As Malhar is becoming his own man, I find myself having a hard time with it.. He is becoming more independent and I am feeling scared because I am afraid he isn't prepared for the real world. . Despite my encouragement for him to be more independent, proactive, and in charge of his own things, when he really began doing so, I became anxious and worried since he was no longer turning to me for guidance or answers when making certain decisions. When he was displaying the selfassured, take-charge attitude that I was teaching him to act and be, I was taken aback and worried that he would make mistakes and act hastily in his decisions. It wasn't until he and I sat down one day, and I brought up to him about his independence he was displaying that I started feeling comfortable again. Since Malhar was around two or three years old, we have been going to lunch together almost every Saturday together just me and him. This was our time together to catch up and discuss what he was doing in school and how he was getting along with friends and people and it was our bonding time. I crazily would stress if I was not going to be in town on a Saturday if I had to travel for work. This was our time and it meant the world to me. I have always had a crazy busy schedule ever since I could remember, so the 2-3 hours we would spend just the two of us together was precious and most important to me. I knew at some point in life Malhar would want to spend that Saturday doing something else eventually with his "boys" like he likes to call them or with a girlfriend at some point. I would move mountains if I could be home around lunch time each Saturday just to be with him. On one of regular lunch Saturdays at his favorite wing spot, I decided to tell him how I was feeling now that he is showing his maturity and independence in his decision-making process and take-charge attitude towards certain things. I first congratulated him for his independence and told him how proud I am to see him maturing in front of me and how proud his mama would be of her baby boy. He was shocked that I even brought it up and that I recognized it because when he would tell me that he is following the Ramcharran's Rules and embracing our 11 life lessons I would usually not make a big deal about it because I tell him it is what he is supposed to do as a good person, and he would hem and haw but eventually he would say "you are right dad." But this day I was totally different because for the first time I was the one having to discuss the topic and I was not handling it really good well, but he recognized that I was emotional about him becoming his own man and taking charge of his responsibility responsibilities and life decisions and he was very appreciative that we would have has this talk. But what I think he didn't realize that by him recognizing I am acknowledging this milestone he made me feel better and he comforted me that he is getting prepared for the real world and that my efforts were being accepted and appreciated.

Dad's experience:

Being your own man was one of my dad's favorite message to me and my siblings while growing up. He always said you need to be your own person for your own path in life and don't let anyone tell you otherwise. My experience with being my own man was epic I believe. I was told I would never be able to work on my master's degree while still being a fulltime active duty in the Army where I spent 4 years active duty and 11 in the reserves. While everyone was told to take one class at a time because of all the long hours we were required to work as Military Police Officers on the base. The counselors insisted that taking more than two classes would lead to me dropping out of the program because of the difficulty of the subjects and the work requirement to complete the courses. I remember distinctly sitting with the educational officer telling me "lieutenant you will be sorry if you took a full load while in the Army fulltime." Well I begged to differ because I knew I was in for 4 years and I had already served two years and if I wanted to have my advance degree before I left the Army I needed to take a full load even if I was attending school at night. I made an executive decision not to do what the rest of the pack was doing and to enroll as a fulltime student and attend night school with a different class every day of the week including some weekends. I figured out how to do it. I studied diligently and utilized all my free time. I woke up early one extra hour every day and studied to review my course work. I hired a person to help me with researching topics to help reduce time spent on things that consumed what I believe was waste of my time. I partnered with others to help me better understand topics that were new to me, so I had someone to go to when I needed help in that class. Believe it or not everyone was happy to help because they wanted the help as well. I was used to working in a team environment so partnering with others in my class was a tremendous help, since I was taking courses through the military there was a tremendous amount of resources on the post to help military students enrolled in programs especially in the masters and PhD programs, so I utilized all the resources at my disposal. I am happy to say I finished my masters on time in fact one semester early because I was able to dual enroll for one class which helped a lot in finishing. My goal was to graduate with my masters before I left the Army and that happened because I decided to be my own man and take the risk of doing it on my own way and not follow the crowd. Sometimes you must make a decision that is not popular or expected and at the same time just be focused while seeing things through.

Chapter 8

~~~~~~~~~~~~~~~~~~~~~~

Never be afraid to say I am wrong.

Ever since I was young, I was told I was intelligent when it came to knowledge and it escalated my desire for more of it and to learn more. With my entire mind set on learning, I always make sure to constantly ask questions about everything and anything. Sometimes I may ask things that sound redundant Although, just like everyone else, I mess up on occasion and do something that makes me seem dumb or I turn out to be wrong because of my zest for discussion. My parents always told me to "Stop and think before you speak" when it came to analyzing things, but they placed more emphasis on telling me to "Calm down and ease your mind" anytime I would overthink something. whenever I would overthink anything. When I was in my last year of middle school (eighth grade), I was in a bit of a tight situation with a few of my peers. Someone apparently had been messing with my personally assigned desktop in the computer lab by scattering my files and projects everywhere. This happened because we all shared a single account to each computer rather than single personal accounts even though we had those for other websites. I was fuming mad because I worked extremely hard on my coding project and notes, so I didn't take it too well when they were all out of place. I did something that even surprised me at the time; I started to accuse the peers I didn't get along with of tampering with my work while I was out sick since I was out the week before. Unfortunately, I did not get anywhere with that because all I did was make people upset because I didn't have any real evidence other than

their interactions with me. Eventually my computer science teacher stepped in to calm me down and resolve the issue. She offered to show me the camera footage from last week and I took it. It turned out that someone else I knew from the class before us decided to mess with my files as a way of getting revenge on me for getting him caught stealing from the school store. I was really upset about what happened because I let my emotions get the best of me because I didn't want to be wrong since I'm so used to being right. I did not have the intention of personally attacking anyone and making them feel awful, I just wanted to know what happened to my work and I wanted it back to how it was.. Soon after, I apologized to the people I accused of wronging me. Some of them forgave me and blew it off like it was nothing, and we eventually became friends surprisingly. A couple not so much. They either didn't care, didn't want to hear it, or just got more upset at me. I learnt to not fear being wrong and how to admit it, regardless of the result. Eventually admitting to your wrongdoings can make you one of the correct people.

LESSON EIGHT

~~~~~~~~~~~~~~~~

Never be afraid to say "I'm wrong"

"We are full of weakness and errors; let us mutually pardon each other our failures– Voltaire

Malhar's experience:

When I was in the third grade I was pretty much on a roll and was a master at multiplication. When we had a multiplication facts 1-12 test to see who can master the 1-12 times table, I would tell my Dad my score. It was usually 100% all the time. But when I got to level 8 I started to struggle and get nervous on the time and problems. I ended up failing the test which meant I had taken the 8 times table again next week. When I went home my dad asked me how it went on the test. Well instead of saying I failed I said, "I got it all right." Well I failed the 8 times table the next week and I did the same thing again. Saying, "I got it all right." But he found out that I failed. I told him that I was afraid to say that I was wrong because I was embarrassed that every single one of my classmates would be hard on me. After that experience I learned not be afraid to say that you're wrong which should be right.

CHAPTER 8

Never be afraid to say I am wrong.

I believe that we all have to learn and accept that we should admit when we are wrong or when we are sorry. The lack of understanding this is one that will haunt you and tie you up into bondage. If you can never bring yourself to say you were wrong or sorry to a loved one, stranger, a colleague or a friend then you will be empty for the rest of your life.. It will be challenging to maintain long-lasting relationships in your life if you are unable to demonstrate to others that you were mistaken. This is because such a person will lack consciousness and the ability to demonstrate empathy to another human being. Finding one true friend is hard enough but imagine how difficult it would be if you planned to be in a long-term relationship, such as a marriage. A prime example with this - I had a knock down drag out disagreement with Malhar regarding what I thought and felt was a bad attitude and behavior towards another family member. I only got one side of the story so I decided to confront Malhar about his behavior and how he responded in the particular manner he did which I felt was very rude and disrespectful to his elder. After calming down, I sat down with Malhar to hear his side of what happened. I was surprised to learn that this wasn't how the situation actually played out, and Malhar's aunt supported his explanation of what happened and I became agitated and that led me to react the way that I did. After getting Malhar's side of the event and getting more information from his aunt on what actually happened, I felt horrible that I spoke to him the way I did and was going to ground him for a week. I had to eat my words and no parent wants to admit they made a mistake and they were wrong for speaking in a harsh tone or in an aggressive manner to their child. When I recognized I had my facts wrong and I was wrong in my response and behavior I quickly apologized to Malhar for my actions and behavior. Being the sweet child and son, Malhar says "it's okay dad" you are human you can make mistakes too. All I could do was laugh and smile and give him a big hung hug for being so sweet. I didn't want to carry any burden in my heart and when I recognized in that moment, I was wrong I apologized, and it made me feel better and most importantly it made Malhar feel better too.

Dad's Experience:

I am happy to say this was a lesson I learned early and often because my parents were telling me that it is best to say I am sorry and I am wrong. I was hard headed when I was kid, so I had to say I am sorry a lot while growing up. The one event that left a lasting impression on me was when I had to say I am sorry to my brother even though I did not want to because he was younger, and I was certain I was right but that was not the case.

My little brother Bruce, a little trouble maker when we were young. He was 4 years younger and he was notorious for making trouble for me and doing things that would get him in trouble with my folks. He used to take my toys out of my room and play with them and sometimes even give it away to kids who did not have much to play with. Well on this one occasion I was 12 and he was 8 at the time. I went to the ball field with my friends to play softball for a few hours and I left him home with my baseball cards that we were playing with. Back then we used to trade baseball cards and try to win them from the other kids in the neighborhood. I had just bought the very popular Ron Guidry card. He was the ace pitcher at the time I was growing up for the New York Yankee's. I was super excited that I got that card which every one of my friends wanted for their collection. When I left home that card was in room on the dresser and my brother and I was looking at the stats on the back. However, when I returned several hours later that card and the rest of my cards was gone. I was very upset to find out that all my cards were gone and the only person who was playing with them was him and when they were missing I accused him of taking them and giving them away like he was known to do from time to time. I was so upset and angry that I wanted to fight my brother which was not good, now that I look back on it, but at the time I was flushed with anger and emotions. I went right away and told my mom that Bruce took my cards and gave them away. He was also upset that I was accusing him of taking my stuff that he started crying as well. He kept saying it was not him and he didn't know anything. It was a mystery that my all baseball cards had disappeared in thin air. I was not buying it at all.

As soon as my dad came home I told him what happened, and I insisted that Bruce did it. Dad said let's review the situation to get to the bottom of the lost card I said I know Bruce took them and gave them away and he said no he didn't do it. A Few hours went by with no progress of finding any of my cards. I searched my room, the play room and the entire house and had no luck. The next day when my sister came home from her sleep over at our cousin's house I told her what happened and that I was missing my baseball card collection. She was like I took them off your dresser to show my cousin who was a huge Yankee fan as well. She said I was gone so she could not ask me to take them, so she just grabbed them and left without saying anything. I was happy to get my cards back, but I felt so terrible that I accused my little brother who was innocent. My Dad and Mom said you need to tell your little brother that you were wrong to accuse him and to say I was wrong for treating him so bad and making him feel sad even though he did not do anything wrong. I told him right away and he was happy that I admitted I was wrong. As for my sister, my mom and dad told her she should not take things without asking.

Chapter 9

~~~~~~~~~~

What does not kill will fatten.

I used to sort of have this idea of being a perfectionist at everything. It was not necessarily a bad thing, I just had to learn that I did not need to perfect everything. I had to at least have it work or look acceptable.. When it came to accomplishments, I had to learn about trial and error. Not everyone gets it right the first time, and they grow from their past experiences. If you never experience failure, you'll most likely never develop as a person since you won't understand why other people have strengths and weaknesses. You most likely won't be able to draw any

What doesn't kill will fatten (Failure makes you stronger)

conclusions from your own position. When I was around the age of fifteen and sixteen, I had to test for my driver's license. I had already gotten my permit for passing the online test questions about the rules of the road, signs, patterns, actions, safety, hazards, and parking, so I was pretty much all set and ready for the driver's test. I was a bit nervous about the whole experience because it was a big step for my future but also since it cost a bit to retake it and I did not want to do what I believed was time wasting. I took the driving test and sadly missed the last few points needed to pass and receive my license. I was not too happy about failing the test and was making an unnecessarily big deal about it. My father soon approached me and told me that I did not have to worry about not passing and it will happen next time, since they pointed out the flaws in my driving. He said that I'm learning and growing when I fail stuff because there is always an opportunity to try again. When I took my second attempt at the driving test, I passed with flying colors, and got my license. I realized I did not have to push myself to perfect everything, especially since I'm not some high-ranking official that's meant to set an example as a role-model yet but I understand I should always try to do my best and learn from my mistakes. So, I have learned to try and take things at a more normal pace and learn if I mess up what the errors were so I don't make the same mistakes again.

LESSON NINE

"What doesn't kill will fatten (Failure makes you stronger)"

"If you can't make a mistake, you can't make anything"–
Marva Collins

Malhar's Experience:

When I was in second grade I had a lot of science projects, but I pretty much failed them all. Mostly because I didn't understand them or the way they were meant to be made. Well I was upset that I failed them all. I was very irritated because I just didn't know what went wrong. Looking back, I thought I was going to have to redo the second grade. That's when I ran over to Dad for help I told him I didn't want to keep failing things I didn't know. That's when he told me that it was a good that I was failing at first, I thought he was kidding but he said he wasn't. He told me even though I wasn't getting good grades and failing my projects, I couldn't always be successful. He said failure is just the beginning and what you must do is not take all of the times you end up failing so hard and what you should do is focus on what worked and leave behind every little thing that went wrong completely but still look in to it for answers and don't leave everything to waste. Once that was all settled in, I finally was able to do all my projects right and pass through the second grade.

CHAPTER 9

~~~~~~~~~~

What does not kill will fatten

For some reason every time something did not go the way I wanted it to turn out and I would come across as whining, my dad would love to tell me "what does not kill will fatten" and smile at me. It was obviously his attempt to say life experiences is a good thing and the more you fail or face challenges the closer you will get to finding your success. At an early age, I wasn't aware enough to understand what he meant. He was trying to let me know life has ups and downs and we have to develop a sense of learning to cope with disappointments; but now as an adult and a parent of grown children it is very clear to me that experiences that has to do will failure and set up backs is not necessarily a bad thing. It teaches us how to have emotional intelligence and gives us perseverance, which is something I firmly believe is missing in today's society and younger generation. We have lost sight of what is really important for our children and loved ones' emotional development as individuals because we have become so preoccupied with making sure they don't experience disappointments. Without some failures and setbacks, we cannot develop as people or as a society, but it is more important to teach them how to overcome failures, setbacks, and disappointments. "What does not kill will fatten" is something I truly believe in today and I have constantly preached this not only to Malhar a bunch of times but also to his brothers as well and to as many people who will listen to me. Most recently I had to deal with some setbacks in my own business and at the moment, I felt that it was the end of the world at one point but after sitting back and reflecting on the disappointments of potentially losing a large customer, I realized that I was getting complacent and that ultimately could lead us to losing some of our customers business. This lesson taught me and reminded that sometimes we have to experience failure, setbacks and disappointments in order to grow and recognize that we should constantly be striving to be the best and to put forth our best in order to get the desired results we are wanting. I am hoping that Malhar is able to recognize and utilize his disappointments and setbacks as learning experiences so he can become a better individual and that these experiences will prepare him to deal with larger more stressful situations as he progresses in his professional and personal life as a colleague student, husband and perhaps someday as a parent.

Dad's Experience:

What doesn't kill will fatten was my dad's favorite saying. He was my hero growing up, so I took this saying to heart because he was always so in tuned and pleasant when I came to him with my failures and then those words of wisdom would automatically come out of his mouth in the most loving manner. He firmly believed we learned from our failures and he said you should never be afraid to fail it just means you are one step closer to success no matter how many times things didn't work out in my favor. I can remember one specific failure that was a life changing event and if it wasn't for my parent's encouragement I don't know what I would be doing today. When things happen when you are young you think and feel it's the end of the world. I am here to tell you it's not so! Keep your head up.

What I thought was my biggest failure at the time was my failure to get placement into the Army Finance Corp, instead I got slotted to the Military Police Corp, it was my single number one choice for my military career to be a career finance officer. I was so upset that this happened. All I could think of was what a failure all these years working towards becoming a finance officer was a waste of my time. After a pity party and crying session, I called my folks to let them know what happened. My dad and mom said it's not the end of the world, why don't you come home for the weekend it will give you some time to clear your head and eat some home cooked meals. I remember laughing because it changed my focus and it made me feel so much better. When I arrived home that weekend to visit I was greeted with the warmth and love that came with my usual visit but this time my folks were warm but stern about my situation what I called a failure my dad said his favorite saying, "what doesn't kill will fatten" I immediately went on the defense saying I worked so hard it is not fair. The talk about that life wasn't fair soon came but what followed afterwards changed my whole outlook. My dad asked me now that you are assigned to the Military Police Corp does it mean you will not serve your country? I was like of course not I joined Army Officer Corp because I wanted to serve the country and possibly have a career. It then dawned on me, he was right that it was not the end of the world that I didn't get what I wanted but it may be an entirely new opportunity that I did not even consider. I am happy to say that today looking back on the situation it may have been a blessing in disguise. The lesson was it was just a setback in the grand picture of my life. It didn't kill me, and it made me stronger for that today it has helped with my life success.

Chapter 10

~~~~~~~~~~~~~~~~~~~~~

Hell, and Heaven is right here on earth.

When my mother passed away, it brought me to my absolute lowest point and most depressing part in my life. It was very traumatic to lose my mother. It left an emotional scar and has had a very strong impact on my life. If I was alone with no one else by my side, I probably would have struggled even more with coping and grieving with her passing and probably lose the will to continue. Luckily I was not alone, I had my family, especially my father. He told me we had

to be strong and continue to make our way through life no matter what gets in the way to try to stop us, saying that we have to make the most of today and live now or never. "Heaven and Hell are right here on Earth- make the most of today!" father tells me. I still remember the good memories of my mother fondly, even if there were some not so good ones towards the end seeing her in pain and struggling to be well. I know I will never forget my mother or take anyone in my family for granted ever because we have to make the most of our life daily. Everyone's time comes eventually, so we must make the most of everyday we have in this life. If we don't do so we will have hell on this earth.

LESSON TEN

"Hell, and Heaven are right here on Earth"– Make the most of today

When you focus on being a blessing, God makes sure that you are always blessed in abundance.

Joel Osteen

Malhar's Experience:

When I was in the fourth grade I had terrible grades that my father always got on me and my mother was on me too. I ended up having to go to after school for tutoring but still even then I could hardly improve, and I was super upset about what would happen on Florida Standards Assessment (FSA). Things weren't looking good for the semester and I was getting so nervous that I thought I'd end up failing the 4th grade or even worse, fail school itself. I thought my mind was making itself up that I didn't have to live yet, and I had to live later. I told my father that I was going to end my life and restart, but he told me "NO." I thought he was joking. "If you're going to live you need to live now not sooner or later." he said to me "You have so much to live for." I then understood what he was saying. If I want to live I need to live now or else never. I was still upset about my grades and I told him I wanted to get them fixed, so he and my mother offered to help me so when the second semester started I got As and Bs and I passed the fourth grade and made it to the fifth grade. I even did better on the FSA. But I do want to say that I did not really appreciate how school was making me feel but I do know it's for my own good and I know it's pretty big work, but I know one day I'll make my whole family proud and all my friends and enemies jealous. But don't forget to live now or never, hell and heaven are right here on Earth with us.

CHAPTER 10

～～～～～～～～

Heaven and Hell is right here on Earth– Make the most of today!

Hell, and Heaven is right here on earth. "Hell, and Heaven is right here on earth" is a very philosophical way of looking at life and perhaps at times when I was trying to explain and in part this life lesson to Malhar and his brothers it may have not always stick or translate as I wanted it to. but now that Malhar is older and becoming more aware and mature, I truly believe he gets it. Since we originally released the first edition of this book, we have had to deal with a number of situations that we can apply this life lesson to Malhar's mom passing a way away the way she did served as a prime example for both of us experiencing what we would say heaven and hell is in this earth. We both recognized that having your loved one around you all the time should not be taken for granted. When Sadhana was around, we were always feeling happy and comforted because that's what moms do, they make us feel like we are the best in the world and we are the light of their eyes. Malhar loved his mom immensely and he does miss her a lot and when she passed it was like our world came crashing down and now our heaven turned to hell. It was like what happened? How could this beautiful life get turned upside down in a matter of moments! We all had to deal with a tragedy and learn to accept that this was happening to us and there was nothing we could do to change it. Eventually the pain gets less over time but never goes away. No one wants always to always feel as if they are drowning in pain or constantly feeling despondent and there is no hope; this is when we have to remember that your heaven is still on earth and that we have to learn to cope and deal with setbacks, hurt, pain and loss so we can enjoy this life and live in a joyful and meaningful manner no matter what happens or is thrown into your pathway. Malhar dealt with his obstacles and tragedy as best as a parent would expect. He has been an inspiration to me and his family with continued focus on being a better student and working towards improving himself as a young man. He has experienced challenges as well as setbacks, but he has come to realize that "Hell and Heaven is right here on earth," and that how we respond to each situation in life will ultimately affect how we feel. He also understands that we can make our lives as wonderful as we want them to be by focusing on the things we can control rather than worrying about the things we cannot.

Dad's Experience:

Growing up one of the other important lesson my parents use to drill into our head was "Heaven and Hell is right here on Earth." It simply translated to meaning to live your life to the fullest because you have today for certain tomorrow is not promised. Dad was very persistent that we did our very best each and every time no matter how big or small the event or project was. My first recollection of this lesson was when I around 7 or 8 years old. My parents always wanted us to study and engage in events and programs that will help us become better students, so my dad signed me up for the chess club at our catholic school that my sister and I attended. My first day at the chest club was awful because I did not how to play at all and everyone there was older, and they already knew the game. I was not liking it at all. The only thing I could do during that first day was say why am I being subjected to this torture to learn a game with all these funny pieces up until this point I was playing go fish and chutes and ladders and monopoly on occasions when my cousins came over. I came home that day and told my dad I did not like that club and I wanted to switch to basketball club instead and he said you have to make the most of this opportunity because he had to ask a favor to get me into that club since it was for older kids and he wanted me to get a head start. I was like why, he gave me the look and I said never mind I hear you. He said again it's the opportunity you have and that I needed to take advantage of it now not later because it would take another two years to get in that club and benefits of learning chess will be priceless. I was like this was not fun at all. After about a month of going for lessons and making new friends who were older it became apparent to me I was in a good place I was meeting older kids and hanging around them while my other friends were jealous that the older kids knew who I was and talked to me in the hallways. I then figured out what dad meant by taking advantage of all the opportunity even if it's hard at the time.

Live your life from a position of abundance.

When I think something to be abundant in my own life, I often think about how many times I could have lost something simple to get but that required investing time, space, and/or money. I was pretty generous growing up and still try to be without giving into selfish desires. I used to be part of this book club in middle school. We would talk about whatever books we were assigned to us during the school year and whatever we chose to read outside of school. I had a couple friends in the little book club, and we sometimes would trade, share, and borrow books with one another. Close to the end of one of our little club

meetups, one of my friends borrowed my Harry Potter books and asked me if he could borrow it for a little longer. I told him I'd ask my mom when it was time to leave. Unfortunately, my mother didn't approve since it was actually my brother's book and he also wanted it back eventually. My friend got a bit persistent on giving it back, tightening his grip on the book. He looked pretty devastated that I had to take it away from him by force. I wanted to convince my parents to let me give him a used copy online as a present. After getting their approval and buying the book. I brought the book and gave it to him on Monday. I like to think that what I did was kind and generous and it left me to live a more abundant life. As I am growing older and having more life experiences I realize I live a gifted life and have learned not to take things for granted.

LESSON ELEVEN

"Always live your life from a position of abundance"

"I've had a lot of worries in my life, most of which never happened." Mark Twain

Malhar's Experience

When I was 6, I just wanted a friend who liked the same things as I did that was important at that time and fortunately now I have a best bud now who enjoys the same things. I had a Nintendo Wii system and I had a bunch of games on it like, "New Super Mario Bros" Wii from 2009. One of my father's friends came over for a meeting and he brought his son with him. He asked me if I had a Wii and I said "yes. "The next thing he asked me was if I had the New Super Mario Bros Wii and I said "yes" again. He asked me to show him, so I did. We played up to world level 6. After that he looked at my copy of New Super Mario Bros Wii and he said he really wished he had one of his own. "After a few minutes he had to go, at that moment he refused to give me back my copy of the game. He started yelling and crying and I asked my mom if I could give him the game, she said no because it cost a lot of money" So, I told him to give me back my game or else the next time he came he wouldn't be able to play any other games I had. But he still didn't give it back. So, he forced me to snatch it out of his hands and give it to my Dad and he held it up in the air and his friend's son tried to jump and grab it and I told him to stop and Dad's friend grabbed him and went. That's when I asked my dad if I could order a New Super Mario Bros Wii copy online and send it to Jeremy my Dad's friend son he can give it to him; I knew it was nice on my part despite him being foolish, but I felt bad that he was crying. I like to think I'm a nice guy, so I got it for Jeremy and I sent it to him and we moved on. It's too bad I don't get to see him as much I would like to since they live far away.

CHAPTER 11

Live your life from a position of abundance

"Living your life from a position of abundance" is my daily affirmation and I have thought Malhar this just as my father had thought me and his father did to him. We have embraced this as way of living and looking at the world and what it means to being part of a group, community and even in our family. I will tell you this was not always easy for Malhar to understand as a younger child, but I can tell you today he has learned to really embraced, "live your life from a position of abundance" by becoming a person who is giving, loving, and unselfish with his time, love, sharing and finally learning how important it is to volunteer your time. We have never had to worry too much about him wanting to share his stuff because every child goes through the "mine" stage. When he reached his teenage years, however, he began to realize and understand that not everyone has the same academic abilities and lives in the same privileges as him, and that by living his life from a position of abundance he will be able to better understand the world around him and not to take his life for granted. He has learned it first-hand that one's life can drastically change forever in just a few minutes and that when you can see your life as being abundant you will never really feel the need to be arrogant and rude to others. He has had his moments, believe me but once he is given a little reminder it falls back in line with this lesson of living from a position of abundance. I have had to remind myself most recently that I need to "live your life from a position of abundance." I guess everyone at some point needs to be reminded that we can't always get what we want when we want it and that sometimes things are not meant to be. and once we can learn to accept it; you will feel better and not have to stress about things that are not in your immediate control. It does not mean we won't ever get what we want or desire, but maybe we have not done all what's needed to acquire that desired outcome or want and perhaps we need to continue to work smarter or harder to get that goal accomplished. I tell Malhar and the family all the time we are blessed, and we have all we need to be happy, productive and to have a meaningful existence in this lifetime. I truly believe if we all learn to "Live your live from a position of abundance," We can truly have a stress-free, quality life.

Dad's Experience:

I believe of all the sayings and lessons my dad had I strongly believe this one has had the most lasting impact ever. Dad taught me and my two siblings some super life lessons that has shaped our life and now I have passed it on to Malhar and his other brothers. Living from a position of abundance is a guide to help you make good decisions when it comes to interacting with others and how you would want to be treated and how to make good life and intelligent decisions. This lesson is a full proof way to never cheat or harm another individual no matter what the circumstance is. If you take a moment and break it down its so simple and true. What it translates to is live your life as if you have no need in the world and when you can get to that point the universe lines up and good things happen to you. Always remember there is someone else out there in more need than you and if you can see that you will never need to take short cuts in your life because you are not pressed in to make a bad decision or cheat anyone you come in contact with.

Here is a great example of living from a position of abundance that most everyone can relate to. When I was a kid, I could remember that I really wanted a car racing set called TCR "total control racing" it was the hottest toy back in the late 1970's and early 80's. I convinced my dad to get that for me for Christmas and like always he never disappointed. Christmas morning it was under the Christmas tree I was totally excited that I got what I wanted, that evening one of my mom's co-workers came by to visit our house to pick up some items my mom had for her. While visiting she had her 6 years old son with her and like most kids during Christmas he was excited to play with new toys after visiting and playing with my Total control racing toy, it was time for him to leave with his mom, but he refused to give me back my toy. He started crying and screaming when his mom was trying to take it away from him. He kept saying I didn't get anything for Christmas and that he really liked my toy. After some time, he still continued to scream. I went over to my dad and ask if I could let him take the toy I was hoping to get for Christmas and I loved the most out of all the items I had gotten for Christmas. I was too young to know at the time that they weren't as well off as I were, but I wanted to let that kid have my favorite toy because I saw how happy he was when he was playing with it. It was the first time I really understood what my dad was saying about live from a position of abundance. What was interesting the following day when we went to my favorite uncle's house to visit my cousins under the Christmas tree was a gift for me and when I opened it up it was a TCR car racing set just like the one I let the little boy take with him. It was that exact moment I knew and felt what my dad was saying to me. I lived it and it came full circle in my favor. Ever since then I have tried my very best to live my life from a position of abundance.

Epilogue

This book teaches real life lessons through the eyes of a 11-year-old and his father.

Lesson one teaches you to never give up, be persistent to achieve your goals. Lesson two and three teach you that procrastination does not give you the best results. Lesson 4, leaders make things happen for themselves and others. Lesson five teaches you that you are responsible for your own choices and decisions. Lesson 6 teaches that you cannot drive while looking through rear-view mirror for you to move ahead keep looking forward and you'll make great progress make. Lesson 7 teaches you to make your own decisions and don't get influenced negatively. Lesson eight teaches you to accept your mistakes and to learn from them so you don't make them again. Lesson 9 says don't worry about mistakes and injuries they make you stronger and learn from them last. Lesson 10 live your life to the fullest make it heaven not hell. Lesson 11 teaches us there is more pleasure in giving than receiving.

By Sadhana Ramcharran

About the Authors

Malhar Ramcharran & Dr. Ram Ramcharran decided to write these short stories and life lessons as a way to help share similar experiences they had while growing up; since Malhar encountered some bullying from classmates in middle school at the time; Dr. Ram wanted him to write down his experiences as way to help him better understand what was happening at school. Dr. Ram also encountered some similar events while growing up in New York City. He didn't want Malhar to feel he was alone, so he encouraged him to write about his feelings and thoughts to help him better understand what was happening; while using the encounters that they shared with each other's as life lessons to better understand the experiences they both shared.

Malhar was 12 when the first edition of this book came out. He is now 18 years old and attends a STEM Fundamental High School which focuses on Science, Technology, Engineering and Math which are subjects he really enjoys. Malhar loves digital animation, art, technology, coding, Minecraft games and writing. He wants to someday own and run his own Digital Animation company. In the meantime, he is creating content on YouTube for his work and is sharing his videos and lessons to other children as a way to help them feel better about themselves and to help them cope with bullying. Malhar will be attending Full Sail University in their accelerated BS to MS Program in the Fall of 2024.

Dr. Ram P. Ramcharran is a Clinical Psychologist, Businessman, Entrepreneur, and the author of several self-help books. He decided to write this book with Malhar to help him better understand the experiences he was having during his adolescent years and to use it as a way to bond with him; and to make understand the lessons he has shared and talked about since he was 2 years old. Dr. Ram wanted Malhar to know these are not just words but there are actions behind it that would help Malhar and others like him who are encountering similar experiences. Dr. Ramcharran is extremely proud of Malhar for wanting to share his lessons with others despite them being so personal. They recognized it may help others work through similar challenges that Malhar encountered and faced. Malhar and Dr. Ram Ramcharran live in Tarpon Springs, Florida.

Self Help/Inspiration

A Father and Son's Journey is Love and understanding for each other and the people around them. Malhar and Dr. Ram Ramcharran live what they taught in this book. I know that the short stories and lessons they shared comes from the center of their hearts. I have seen it and experienced their love and compassion for each other and the people around them.

Dr. Shelton Wood. Jr.– GWUA President

Reading the stories of the lessons shared between a father and son brought back most the wonderful memories I had with my dad growing up in Atlanta, GA. This is a wonderful way these life lessons were shared about growing up and some of the challenges faced by children. I encourage everyone to pick up this book and share it with your loved ones.

Philip Nelson– Senior Vice President – Wells Fargo Wealth Managements

www.ingramcontent.com/pod-product-compliance
Lightning Source LLC
Chambersburg PA
CBHW051232120626
46547CB00013B/1615